The Relationally Driven Approach

By

Dwayne Castle

www.relationallydriven.com

© 2018 Dwayne Castle

All rights reserved. No portion of this book may be reproduced in any form without written permission from the publisher, except as permitted by U.S. copyright law. For permissions contact:

contact@relationallydriven.com

Cover by Dwayne Castle

ISBN 978-1-9802-1439-7

Table of Contents

Introduction
Page 3

Chapter One
The What & Why of Relationally Driven
Page 8

Chapter Two
People Matter
Page 19

Chapter Three
You Matter, Too
Page 38

Chapter Four
Authenticity Matters
Page 54

Chapter Five
Bringing It All Together
Page 61

Epilogue
Page 70

Introduction

I could not believe my ears. My employee had actually asked me "why?!" I remember thinking- "you've got to be kidding me, 'why?' is not a proper response to a given order."

Up to this point in my life the question "why" only traveled in one direction and that was down the chain of command. "Why didn't you turn your homework in on time?" or "Why did you run that stop light?" or "Why did you stick that crayon up your nose?" It never travelled in an upward manner.

My father had been in the Army during The Cold War and worked with missile defense systems. "Why" was not an optional response when given a military command and he reiterated that at home. His answer to "why" came in the form of a butt whooping, so I learned to not ask why.

When I served in the Navy during Desert Storm, that lesson was reinforced. From a paraphrased snippet of the old poem by Tennyson, "mine is but to do or die, not to ask the reason why." You can ask "how" to do something and you can ask "when" that something needs done. You can ask for a clarification because you don't understand the "what." But, what you can't do, what you must never do, is ask "why."

In every area of my life I had been taught that orders are orders which must immediately be obeyed, (or else). So, now you can understand my disbelief at being asked "why" my employee had to do what I had instructed her to do.

There I was, the new group lead for the customer service department of a multi-million dollar portrait publishing company and my employee was questioning me and apparently my authority.

I gave the obvious answer, the one that perhaps you the reader may have given; the one that millions of parents give every day and the one that millions of kids swear they'll never say when they grow up; "Because, I said so!" Of course, most of those kids grow up, repeat that phrase, and follow up quickly with "Oh no! I've become my parents."

"Because I said so" was not the appropriate response. I know this because it landed me in the office of the Human Resources Manager who said "Dwayne, 'because I said so' was not the appropriate response." I was further informed that instead of "because I said so" I needed to get "buy in" from my employees.

"Buy-in" was a new phrase for me in this context; we weren't playing poker. I challenged the notion on the grounds that we, as the employer, had purchased the "buy-in" by giving the employee the privilege to work there and a paycheck.

I was basically met with, "how's that working out for you?" Up to this point, it had worked well but I had to admit that my way didn't seem to be working in this environment and that if I expected different results I needed a different approach. I was then given strict orders to find another way.

Since I had already made the case that "why" should never be directed upward in the chain of command, I bit the bullet. I decided that I had a choice to continue operating from my own understanding, perspective, and preferences or to explore a different way of approaching those I was leading. I made it my mission to find a solution and to make my way in this new alternate reality in which I had suddenly found myself.

That was my "aha" moment where dilemma required solution. Maybe that's where you are right now, wondering why you aren't receiving the results that you've been expecting or have previously experienced. Maybe you realize that what you are doing is ineffective and what may have worked before, isn't working now- if it ever worked in the first place.

Your aha moment could have come like mine in the HR managers office or over time as you realized that your sales numbers aren't moving in the right direction, the morale of your associates is sliding, or your regular customers aren't quite as regular as they once were.

On the personal level you could be aware of an increase in the volume and intensity of the arguments you are having with those you love or the level of detachment from those closest to you. Personal relationships can make the biggest impact on your success journey and if you're struggling with how to relate there, it most certainly carries over into every other role you play in life.

Whatever it is that led you here, the beauty is that in my quest to improve my leadership style on the job, I discovered principles that apply to work, home, volunteer efforts, and every other area of my life. Every role I have benefits from being intentional about my approach to others.

That word "principle" is a pretty big deal. When I am Relationally Driven as a way of life I have greater satisfaction, fulfillment, and success. When I disregard the principles and rely on the old stand-by of responding by emotion, I find myself and my relationships in a struggle.

As you continue reading, I will share with you the perspective changes that are necessary in order to live relationally. I'll also show you why living relationally changes not only your life but the lives of those around you, for the better.

I'll share with you why you can't simply apply pieces and parts of this methodology and expect sustainable success. But I'll also share how making small and subtle changes in your approach can and will move you and your vision in the right direction, while helping to propel others into their destiny. Everybody wins!

As you read, the motivations behind each of your relationships will be challenged. The groundwork will be laid for you to evaluate every encounter in which you find yourself. You may feel like you are doing okay, but like a car that seems to be operating well, a little fine tuning and tweaking in your approach to others will help you to operate on a more efficient level and deliver a more satisfying ride, relationally speaking.

Using these Relationally Driven principles, I have trained call center employees how to work with customers in ways that helped to cut refunds by half, increase reorder sales averages, and improve overall customer satisfaction. I've used the same principles in the debt-collection industry, becoming a top-tier collector and trainer, without the harsh, forceful and bullying tactics that the industry has become known for.

These principles have helped to establish teams of people who are filling the needs of those less fortunate. Locally and globally; we provide food and clothing to those in need, disaster relief buckets for those affected by hurricanes, water wells for those with no access, support and materials for schools, as well as providing other comforts, encouragement, and prayer for those in need.

These principles have led to me being a better husband, father, grandfather, friend, employee, and leader and they can do the same for you. I invite you to join me as I share a different way of looking at each of the relationships you have, and how living according to this Relationally Driven Approach, as a principle, will not only position you for success but quite possibly help you redefine what success means to you.

◆◆◆

Chapter One
The What & Why of Relationally Driven

Impact and Destiny

Be it the profitability of a department or a business, the spiritual and emotional growth of a family, or the maturing of our dreams from seed to reality, we are all responsible for some aspect of the fruitfulness of our lives. Those are each a tall order and you can't achieve them alone. You need people and they need you.

This book is about two things- 1) maximizing your impact with people so they realize their value, and 2) how realizing their value gets you closer to your desired destination.

The types of success that you want and that this world needs from you requires good and healthy relationships with the people you encounter along your daily journey.

Whether it is your boss and co-workers, your customers and vendors, your spouse and children, or any of the random people you meet along the way, you have the power to bring out the best in others. When you do, there's a tendency for your best to be brought out as well.

Profitable To Be Around

To answer your question "What is Relationally Driven?" I present this hypothetical: if I gave you $10 every time we were to get together, what would happen? That's right! You would find all kinds of reasons to get together with me.

You would see me on the street and feel the need to say hello. You would invite me out to coffee. You would knock on my door to let me know you just happened to be in the neighborhood. You would probably find many other reasons to bump into me and to bump into me often. And if you were any kind of friend, you would probably bring others along with you in the hopes that they, too, would benefit from connecting with me.

Relationally Driven is living intentionally in such a way that people profit from being in your presence. People tend to like being around others who add to their value. That's human nature and the premise behind this philosophy and this book. How you treat people determines, by and large, their treatment of you and their level of desire to have you around.

Am I suggesting that you start giving away money as a way to win friends and influence people? I suppose that is one way to do it, although it's probably not the most effective. Money isn't always in supply and thankfully it isn't the only way to profit someone or to gauge prosperity for that matter.

Prosperity certainly can include finances. However, when you turn on the news you'll often see millionaire celebrities, pro-athletes, and politicians who have destroyed their lives and their families, their reputations and their legacies. Despite the fact that they had plenty of money they were not living prosperous lives.

That is why I define profit as any increase to a person's well-being, on any level. Prosperity is joyful living with regard to ones created value, physical & mental health, finances, relationships, dreams & purpose, etc.

When a person was unhappy, but are now full of joy they have experienced an increase. When one learns something that has the power to improve the quality of their life, they have profited. When they have been caused to smile, be encouraged, or motivated to do well, they have been made to prosper.

That is where you come in. When you give your time, resources, effort and energy to someone as a means of putting them further ahead, you have added to their value. Demonstrating compassion, empathy or otherwise helping to lighten their burden enriches them.

Any time you cause someone to be in a better frame of mind or better situation; when you cause them to feel better or to be better, in a healthy way, you have prospered them and that is what being Relationally Driven is about.

Sowing & Reaping

My objective with each encounter is to cause the other party to be better off. It's not about people pleasing so that you can win approval and validation from them. It's about filling needs, encouraging others, easing burdens and otherwise helping people advance toward a successful future. And when that happens, we all win!

Stop for a moment and imagine each of your daily roles. What is the potential impact of people recognizing that you have made a deposit into their bank of well-being?

As in the example of giving money to a person every time they bump into you, I submit that the people you cause to prosper tend to like being around you. They look forward to you entering the room or arriving into their situation.

It's been said that people won't always remember exactly what you said or did for them but they will remember how you made them feel. If you make them feel better with each encounter, they will recognize the pattern and repeatedly put themselves into that position. How could this affect your business, your work, or your home life?

I look at it the way a farmer might look at sowing and reaping. If he were to plant one seed it may or may not grow. However, when he plants lots of seeds, he has a confidence that eventually an entire crop will be ready to harvest.

In much the same way, if we plant these seeds of prosperity; encouraging others, filling needs, and helping people, we don't know which ones will grow and which ones won't. But, like the farmer, eventually we will see good things springing up around us.

A difference between a farmer planting seeds and us living with the intention of causing people to prosper is that farmers only have certain seasons available to them and we don't. We can sow seeds all the time. No matter what season of life we are in we can show kindness and compassion.

That's not to say that there aren't seasons where we need kindness and compassion shown to us but that never negates the need for us to have a lifestyle of giving it out. We may not always have as much in us to give but we always have something and when we give out of that, there will be a return.

Farmers are limited to their field but we can plant anywhere. You can walk into your neighbor's field and plant a seed of encouragement. You can walk into the grocery store and plant a seed of generosity.

It would be amazing if we had entire communities full of people walking around profiting each other everywhere they go. Reading and implementing the principles in this book could cause you to be a trend setter where you live and work. Maybe wearing a farmer's bib overalls could, too. (Picture a winking emoji here.)

Farmers tend to know what the crop will look like and when it will be ready for harvest. We don't necessarily know which seed is going to produce which kind of harvest, or when. But we do know that over time at many of those seeds will produce.

We may not be personally impacted by a specific seed, but just like birds and wind may carry some of the farmers seed away, applying Relationally Driven principles can cause a chain reaction of positive impact beyond your own sphere. Just because something doesn't sprout in your field doesn't mean its potential has less value.

From Analogy to Application

Applying this farmer analogy to the business owner, what would it mean to have employees who are encouraged by you? It's been stated time and again that good employees don't quit jobs they quit bad bosses.

Encouraged employees are more likely to be mindful of their performance, to lift the morale of the team, and to treat customers as their reason for having a job in the first place. Relationally Driven employers attract, keep, and multiply quality employees by investing in them with time, effort, and money.

What would it mean to you as the owner or manager of a business to have customers who feel valued when they walk through your doors? As a customer myself, I know when I'm valued and when I'm not.

I don't like going places where the employees are unhappy. They make me feel as if I'm an inconvenience to their day. My friends don't like that either and I know this because we talk. Relationally Driven businesses attract customers who talk about their experience at your brick & mortar in a positive light.

As an employee, what would it mean to your career, finances, and level of job fulfillment to have bosses, co-workers, and customers who appreciate the way you meet their needs and solve their problems?

You don't have to be the most skilled employee but when you are the one that people like having around because of your intentionality toward them, you make personnel decisions like hiring, retention, pay rate, and promotions much easier. Relationally Driven people are more employable, more profitable, and not easily dispensable. Not coincidentally, they are also more fulfilled.

Take the thought further than the work place. As someone who leads a volunteer based organization or some other non-profit entity, how could your reputation as a person who values others help you with your financial goals, recruitment efforts, and overall mission? Relationally Driven people develop a reputation of trust-worthiness that makes it easier for people to willingly and voluntarily give you their time, talent, and treasure.

On the home front, if your mate knew by your actions that you cared more for their well-being than your own, would it impact the emotional temperature of the home?

If you expressed love to your spouse and children, showed interest in their projects, listened to and encouraged them in their hopes & dreams, could it make a difference to their outcomes? Of course it could! Relationally Driven people intentionally put their family ahead of themselves and in turn are put in a position of peace and fulfillment at home.

Of course, not every single person you encounter in your life will appreciate or reciprocate the Relationally Driven Approach. As stated in the farmer analogy, not every seed will grow. I'll address some of this in a future book about how to deal with ungrateful people and toxic relationships. But when you live with the intentionality of always adding to the value of the person in front of you, you will eventually recognize healthy growth surrounding you.

Looking Back to Get Ahead

As I stated in the introduction, my way of dealing with employees was frustrating and ineffective and had caused more than one trip to the office of the HR manager. The resulting challenge from those visits caused me, over time, to evaluate my thinking processes and motivations. It caused me to evaluate not just my approach to employees but my approach to every relationship I was in.

Upon reflection, I realized that much of the leadership model I had experienced previously was based on positional authority. That model may have worked well in the military and police environments, but it had not been effective in non-military environments.

In the civilian work force, in school, or even at home, the "obedience or else" model was likely responsible for more than a few unintended consequences; rebellion and relational distance among them.

I've thought back to the various teachers I'd had in school and realized that I typically gave the bare minimum for those teachers who were harsh, dictatorial or indifferent to me. As a student, if I picked up on the fact that my teacher didn't care (real or imagined), I didn't care either. I could be inattentive, disrespectful, or even disruptive.

Regardless of my childish rebellion and the resultant bad grades, detentions, suspensions, and missed learning opportunities, it could have been avoided if those teachers (and I) were equipped with these Relationally Driven principles.

On the flipside, I think back to my favorite teachers and they were the ones who showed kindness and care. They treated me as an individual with my own personality and life experiences.

Despite my quirks and idiosyncrasies, those teachers were the ones that went out of their way for me and in the process demonstrated that I was worth their time and effort. I gave those teachers my attention and my best efforts. I also learned the most from them.

How about you? Which teachers motivated you the most? Was it the humorless teacher who was always about the lesson plan and teaching to the bell, or was it the one who addressed students individually, with care and compassion?

Did you prefer the teachers who were dry and professional or those who displayed warmth and even some level of transparency? I always connected with the teachers who shared portions of their personal lives with me. They trusted me with that portion of themselves and that trust conveyed the message that they valued me.

Beyond the school environment, I think of the various jobs I've held in my life and readily admit that when I was younger, I did not always give 100% to the tasks before me.

Like my school days, I gave my best when I felt as if the boss or the team cared about me as a person. Sure, I put on a good face and gave adequate effort but I could have given more. In those days, I was certainly motivated more by the bosses I enjoyed being around.

Some may see much wrong with this thought process and they may be right. But the truth is that people tend to perform better when they like the person for whom they are performing.

Minimum production requirements may be met when employees give "just enough" effort to get by with their non-relational bosses. But for those Relationally Driven bosses who demonstrate genuine appreciation of their employees, their teams are usually more than happy to perform with added effort, going above and beyond the minimum.

Through the challenge that my HR manager levied at me those years ago, I learned to harness my past experiences, to be cognizant and to be intentional about how I approach the people in front of me.

Whether on the job, in my home, or on the street, I see people who need the best me. In the next few chapters I am going to share the specific principles I've found necessary for this Relationally Driven perspective.

Chapter Two - People Matter

Drama, Trauma, or Crisis

Every person you encounter has gone, will go, or is going through some challenge in life. Whether that issue is visible to you or ranks as serious or not in your estimation is immaterial because their trouble is their trouble and is very real to them.

By way of example, about 1o years ago, I was almost forty years old and had suddenly found myself alone for the first time in my life. Simultaneously, I found myself in a financial hole, questioning the reason for my existence, and on the verge of some very poor personal choices.

Recognizing my need to make significant changes, I took a job in traveling sales which kept me on the road 3-4 days per week. The hours and the money were great as was the filling of my need for a change of scenery. I needed far less time sitting home, staring at the walls, and contemplating the darkness which at the time was my life.

On a particular week that winter I was tasked with driving from my home in Ohio to small and scenic St. Mary's Pennsylvania, about 250 miles and four hours away from my place. My car broke down a couple of times along the way and I was able to nurse it all the way to my destination where it did in fact die.

It was towed to a local mechanic with the hope that he would be able to revive it while I spent the week working my gig. The assumption was that by the time the long weekend rolled around my car would be fixed and I would head home. As Saturday rolled around my job came to a close for the week. The mechanic advised me that my car would not be ready until the coming Tuesday. Ugh!

This meant several things to me, none of which were good. Because this wasn't work related I was responsible for paying my own food and lodging expenses for the weekend. Between that and the upcoming bill for the car repairs, this business trip was quickly enlarging that financial hole I previously mentioned.

Next, and of biggest concern to me, was that I now had a very long weekend in that hotel room to do what I had attempted to avoid by taking this job in the first place; sitting and contemplating.

I was now going to be forced to confront all that was going wrong in my life, how far removed I was from my original plans, and how I just couldn't seem to catch a break. It was as whiny and pathetic as it sounds but that is exactly where I was in that period of my life.

The prospect of a weekend alone in a hotel room was not at all appealing to me and the signs of a mental breakdown were rapidly approaching me. After talking with a friend on the telephone, I determined that since I am fairly extroverted, I desperately needed to be around people. That would help me get my mind off of my woes.

Because I am a man of faith, I also recognized that I was probably going to be better off around like minded individuals. It was either go to church the next morning or begin the process of making those poor personal choices I was avoiding by being on the road in the first place. Church it was.

I woke up determined to get there and since my car was down, I had to walk, in the snow, uphill, for more than a mile. Not a joke. Yuck. I made the long cold walk and arrived at the church full of hope and the expectation that I would be greeted by spiritual cousins.

It turned out these particular cousins didn't take kindly to strangers. Not only was I not greeted, I was avoided. People intentionally averted their eyes so they would not have to acknowledge my presence. Not one single hello from anyone other than a cursory greeting from the pastor, and of course, he had to say "hi."

The only other "engagement" happened when the pastor instructed the people to shake hands with someone they didn't know. A few of the men seated closest to me approached and offered their hands, shaking mine with no effort or enthusiasm. They flashed very fake smiles and had zero kindness in their eyes. It was painfully obvious that they did not want me in their little club and were only greeting me out of obligation.

I use the word "painfully" because I was genuinely hurt. I was as low in my life as I had ever been. My mind had been racing about all of my failures and woes, and now the people that were supposed to care about me, instead rejected me as a person.

From Rejected to Valued

I left at the completion of that "service" and began the snowy walk back to my hotel room. The longer I walked the angrier I became. As I walked, I saw people entering another church; apparently to enter into service and I had a sudden urge to join them. I fought the urge because there was almost zero chance that I would give anyone else the opportunity to reject me.

I also fought the urge because the sign out front indicated that this was one of those old stuffy churches that belong to an old stuffy denomination that I was warned to stay away from. If anyone would reject me, it would probably be these people.

On the other hand I didn't have anything else to do or anywhere to be. I fought the urge for about a block and half but gave up after determining that I didn't have anything to lose.

I walked up the large stone steps and was met at the door by a little elderly woman. She was probably 4 feet 10 inches tall and close to 125 years old. That may be a slight exaggeration; she was probably closer to 5 feet tall.

She took a step toward me, smiling, and said "Hello, young man, I don't think I know you. Are you new to this church?" I told her that I was just passing through and had been stranded here for the weekend with a broken down vehicle.

She then reached out and gave me the best granny hug that I had ever received in my life. I hope that you know the kind of hug about which I'm referring. It was firm, but not tight. Her tiny arms wrapped around me as far as they could go and gave a gentle but sustained squeeze.

I am not recommending to you that you go around hugging everyone who enters your presence. In the long run, that may not turn out so good for you. But in that moment she was keenly aware of what I needed and in that hug I could literally feel my distress melting away. The anger? Gone. The loneliness? Gone. The rejection? Gone.

I wasn't thinking about my situation, the events that led me to this point, or the people from the previous church who had only moments before missed an opportunity to minister to my needs.

I was thinking about how in this one act of compassion, this lady made me feel as if all was not lost and that I did in fact have a reason for being. Even if everything else in my world seemed to be going wrong, at least I mattered to her.

She offered, since I didn't know anybody, to sit with me and I gladly accepted. As she led me to a seat she introduced me to some of her friends who seemed genuinely happy that I was there, despite the fact that I was just passing through. You can tell when someone is faking and these people were legitimately joyful.

At the end of the service, a couple of people invited me to lunch. On the outside I verbalized a polite "that would be nice. Thank you." On the inside I was jumping up and down in excitement at the prospect of not eating alone.

We went to the local sandwich shop where they bought (yes, they bought) my lunch. We talked about their town and the local industry. We talked about the food. We talked about family demographics. And all of that was exactly what I needed for the moment.

They drove me back to my hotel at which point they gave me a phone number to call if I needed anything at all while I was in town. And they meant it. This was not a hollow gesture.

When I returned to my room and reflected on the day and all that had happened I was amazed. My bank balance hadn't improved, my car was still broken and my overall situation was no different. Yet, everything changed. My spirit was lifted and my whole attitude improved.

I don't typically allow the circumstances of life to get me down but I'm no different than anybody else in that we all have seasons that we go through. We all have moments where we are feeling the pains of loss and loneliness, failure, hopelessness, sickness, struggle, etc.

Those pains had intensified in the moment that I was rejected by people that should have been there for me. And it all turned around on the hug and kindness of a stranger and her friends. One set of people treated me as if I was an intrusion. The other treated me as if I mattered.

That is principle number one; we treat every person we encounter as though they matter because we recognize and treasure their created value.

We don't know what any person is going through at any given time. We don't know the battles going on in their minds or bodies; we don't know the mental, emotional, or spiritual fight they may be in. Seeing their value and treating them accordingly creates the opportunity for you to enhance their value.

It doesn't matter if they are walking through the doors of your church, punching the clock and working alongside you, or waiting on you to cash them out at the bank; the way you treat others, causing them to profit, even in the briefest of moments can make the all the difference in their lives. And, as stated previously, when you plant good things into the people that enter your sphere of influence, your sphere tends to grow good things.

Differences Don't Determine Value

Some people in life have seemingly been dealt a better hand than others. Depending on one's personal accomplishments, the stability of their upbringing, financial well-being, or many other reasons, we can make mistakes regarding the value of ourselves in relation to others.

Negative judgments abound toward people based on things beyond their inherent value. They can be viewed through our own lens of "normal" and if they don't fit that standard, we can determine them as "less than" or "unworthy."

Relationally Driven people look beyond the things that commonly divide others. We look beyond race, religion, and sexuality. We look beyond ideologies, affiliations, and backgrounds. We don't see political parties, financial condition, educational background, family history, or anything else as the determiner of a person's created value.

When we see someone who may be wired a bit differently than we are, we see someone who has value. When we see a person whom others may label as "weird", we see an individual as inherently valuable as any other.

That's not to say that we have to agree with others in terms of their life-choices, thought processes, attitudes, etc. But it does mean that we can't use those things as a means to withhold courtesy, kindness, compassion, justice, etc.

When we puff ourselves up as better than others, or deem them to be "less than" we are, there are dire consequences to the positive impact in our little corners of the world. The very people we see as "different" could very well be the lynch-pin to us reaching our successes and we could be theirs.

When we only see peculiarities in people we are robbed of the benefits afforded by the unique perspectives and experiences that have formed each of us into who we are. When we see inherent worth, it helps us treat people better and in turn, we increase the opportunity to be better people.

It Isn't About the Transaction

When explaining to me about this rough and uncaring world we live in, my father once told me that people have a mindset that "life is cheap, unless it's yours." I would add that many feel their own lives are cheap as well and I'll write more about that in the next chapter.

He was saying that we don't recognize the worth of individuals, on a personal level. We neglect or disregard those that aren't of immediate consequence to us and are careless toward them. We don't, as a society, seem to recognize the real created value of a person- the fact that they matter simply because they exist and should be treated accordingly.

As a whole, we tend to see the transactional value of people. That is, we see them through what I call a WIFM lens, where we make decisions about the worth of others based on "what's in it for me?" *(See figures 1.1 & 1.2 on pages 34 & 35)*

This is a big mistake and it's why marriages and families fall apart. It is why brick and mortar businesses are collapsing in favor of online shopping. It is why society seems to be busting at the seams with entire groups of people rallying and rioting, because the individuals within those groups don't seem to believe they are being seen or heard.

It's in our nature to do cost-benefit analyses on the people who enter into our presence. We tend to look at them in terms of how we think they will benefit us or what they will cost us in terms of time, energy, and resources. We size them up and make split second determinations as to their worth in relation to our agenda.

We see people and treat them as assets and commodities or expenses and liabilities. We see them as tools and as a means to an end or as obstacles that we must go through, over, around or avoid altogether.

But what if we quit valuing people on that transactional level and begin valuing them simply because of their existence? What if we value them because they have their own character and personality? What if we recognize that each person has a story and an experiential reason for their world view? What if we treated them with the understanding that they have hopes and dreams, burdens, hurts, and challenges?

Relationally Driven people approach others from the principle that their existence alone determines that they have value. And we have a mission to add to that value.

The Surrounding Treasures

Think of the impact you could have on your corner of the world, in your home, or at your job, if you treated every single person from the standpoint that they matter and that your objective is to add to their value. Remember, that is the definition of being Relationally Driven- living intentionally in such a way that people profit from being in your presence. *(See figures 2.1 & 2.2 on pages 36 & 37)*

I have friends who scour their community looking for discarded pieces of furniture. They look for the items that others view as worthless or beyond repair, as wastes of space with no value. They find these items on the curb where they've been put for trash removal.

They look at these old dressers, end tables, and wicker chairs to see the natural beauty hidden within and to visualize their potential. After they apply a little tender loving care to the item, careful to bring out its best features and hidden charm, they sell the item for profit. They have become so adept at the process that they have made a decent living in the restoration business. What if we were able to approach people that way?

What if we recognized the presence of inherent beauty, even when it isn't quite so obvious to others? What if we could help them realize their value and maximize their potential? We can! Relationally Driven people intentionally work to bring out the best in others.

Even those people we believe to be a drain have something of value within them. When we recognize this value we can add to it or coax it out of hiding through encouraging words, through time investment, or through any number of ways.

Imagine what it would look like when those people in your sphere of influence get a glimpse of their value and what it would mean for you, your family, your business, your dreams, your relationships when they realize that you've recognized and added to that value.

Who They Are, Not What They Do (or don't do)

Stop for a moment and think about the worth of the people with whom you spend the most time. When you think about their value, what words come to mind? When you get beyond the things they have said or done for you or that offend or bother you, what qualities do you see within them? It may take some time to come up with those words, but it is a great exercise.

For example with my wife Deborah my default mode is to think of the things that she *A) does for me:* supports my endeavors, pleasing to look at, brings me physical and emotional pleasure, etc.; or *B) the things that I don't like in the moment:* she asks me to do chores at inconvenient times, disagrees with me about a spending decision (I mean, really, who could argue with the need for Oreo's), and she falls asleep after hooking me on the Hallmark movie she insisted we watch together, etc.

But when I stop and think about her according to her created value those other things all seem to fade away. I can see her for who she is, not what she does or doesn't do for me. She is an amazingly created individual and over time I've learned that she is sensitive, detail oriented, gifted, faithful, determined, strong, and humble.

Inputs and Outcomes

This is important because one way causes my focus to be about me and my wants while the other causes my focus to be on her and how I can make her life better. In other words, when I see her created value for what it is it causes me to keep her best interests at heart.

When I add to her value, she likes having me around. When I'm selfish and dismissive about her wants and needs, she still loves me but isn't quite as thrilled with my presence. You have to catch this: I'm not putting her ahead so that she will be good to me. I'm putting her ahead because it is my principle to do so.

It doesn't matter if it's a spouse, an employee, a customer, or anyone else for that matter. The motivation behind the approach counts. Putting others first as a means to gain is manipulation and insincerity. Living that way requires masks and fakery which only last so long.

Living principally requires an entirely different way of seeing people. It requires you to be intentional about every encounter, regardless of how insignificant it may seem at the time.

We all have those days where we just can't seem to get it together, where everything we say and do seems to be wrong, and we just look and act like jerks. Even on those days she treats me according to my inherent value. This makes me want to treat her even better, which makes her want to treat me better, which makes me want to treat her better and so on, and so forth.

Marriage is the most obvious example I can use and I'll be delving deeper into The Relationally Driven Approach to Marriage and Family in a future book in this series. But it does highlight the point that when you treat people with an understanding of their value, the stage is set for a mutually beneficial scenario to unfold.

Now remember, just because the stage is set doesn't mean that people are always going to respond as we hope. An intentional lifestyle of being Relationally Driven simply opens more opportunities for positive responses.

Again, it doesn't matter if we are talking about engagement between husband and wife, or between a businesswoman and client, a supervisor and subordinate, a doctor and a patient, or a teacher and a student. When you treat the person across from you according to the principle that they matter, you add more value to their existence and in turn you create more opportunities for better outcomes all the way around.

On the flip-side, when you see the other person only through the lens of what they can possibly do for you or what they have done to you, everyone loses.

When you think about the interactions you have on a regular basis; your family, your customers, co-workers, employees, etc. do those people know you see them for who they are or are they only reminded of what you want and expect from them?

Simply recognizing the value of others is not enough to let them know. Acting on that recognition with our words and deeds is what conveys the message that we appreciate them for that value.

Relationally Driven people don't assume others know our thoughts about their value. We must be intentional about articulating those thoughts verbally and/or with action.

(Figure 1.1)

WIFM People

- ***Inward Focused:*** *What's in it for me?*

- ***Motivated by:*** *Ambition, self-interest, attention seeking, greed & lust.*

- ***Characterized by:*** *Lack of deep relationships. Limited to work related pursuits and relationships or to the gathering of material wealth or status. Giving to gain. More talking to be heard rather than communicating to be mutually understood.*

- ***Frequent use of:*** *"I", "me", "my" and "mine" statements. Asks questions only as a means to improve own circumstance, outcome, or appearance.*

(Figure 1.2)

Additional Qualities of WIFM People

- Engagement with others is based on necessity or as a means to gain.

- Demonstrates kindness with an expectation of reciprocation or acknowledgement. Hurt or offended if people fail to respond "appropriately."

- People are thought worthy or unworthy of one's time, talent, or treasure based on personal bias, prejudice, or expected return.

- Won't forgive those who have caused hurt or offense. Labels their unwillingness to forgive as "inability."

- Unwilling to see others' points of view. Has unkind thoughts, words, & actions toward those with whom they disagree.

- Honors commitments when convenient and beneficial.

- Sees and judges people not as individuals with created value, who have their own life experiences and world-view, but based on the groups with whom they associate. Own sense of morality clouds ability to really see individuals.

- Relational engagement is based on convenience not principle.

(Figure 2.1)

Relationally Driven People

- **Outward Focused:** *How can I best serve you?*

- **Motivated by:** *Principles, convictions, and the needs of others.*

- **Characterized by:** *Deeper relationships and genuine care & compassion for others. Giving with no expectation of return. Communication with the intention of mutual understanding rather than being heard.*

- **Frequent use of:** *Encouraging words as well as questions regarding the needs, desires, and opinions of others in order to benefit them.*

(Figure 2.2)

Additional Qualities of Relationally Driven People

- *Actively seek opportunities to engage with others.*

- *Desire to demonstrate kindness without the need or expectation of reciprocation.*

- *Equally respects people and willing to give time, talent, and treasure regardless of title, position, status. Worthiness is not based on personal biases and prejudices.*

- *Exercises the ability to forgive those who have wronged them.*

- *Desires to see others' points of view and accepts disagreement without de-valuing the individual.*

- *Desires to honor commitments, even to their own hurt.*

- *Sees and respects people as individuals with created value who have their own life experiences and world-view, not based on the groups with whom they associate.*

- *Own sense of morality doesn't cloud ability to see others.*

- *Relational engagement is based on principle, not convenience*

Chapter Three - You Matter, Too

Cogito Ergo Sum
(Or something like that)

As we read in the previous chapter, the very existence of a person indicates that they have created value and if we truly want to be Relationally Driven we must approach them accordingly.

As a preface to the second principle, I quote French philosopher René Descartes, not because I'm super smart and go around quoting philosophers (French or otherwise) but because I ran across him on the Google machine. He is known for writing "I think, therefore I am." Stop and think about that statement for a moment… and by doing so you shall have proven your existence to yourself.

We've already learned that the existence of a person is enough for us to know that they have value. Since you've just proven yours, you must also recognize that you have value. If you have created value you must, as a matter of principle, treat yourself accordingly. Too many people either think too highly of themselves or too little, in relation to the value of others.

Running

I do not like to run. I've never enjoyed running. I didn't mind chasing an ice cream truck now and then but I can drive now so there is no need to run. As part of my grade in gym class I was required to run a mile in a certain amount of time and I had to try every week until I succeeded.

We started off at the beginning of the year with my entire elementary school class running around the school until we hit the one mile mark. If a runner reached the mile in the time allotted he wouldn't have to run again the next week, unless he wanted to beat his time. Can you believe there were kids who actually did that just for fun?

Each week the group of runners got smaller and smaller because only the unsuccessful were required to try again. Did I mention I really dislike running? Weekly, I would have to take the walk of shame to the starting line and weekly, I would take the defeated walk back to the school building knowing what was waiting for me the following week.

Every attempt ended with me running out of steam or finishing but not in the allotted time. But, every week I tried again. Then one week it happened. I did it! Not only did I finish the run but I finished it in the time allowed.

I was excited and even proud of myself and I couldn't wait to tell the people that mattered to me that I had finally done it. Some said "congratulations", some said "they were happy for me", I even got an "I'm proud of you, son" from my mom.

One of the people I couldn't wait to share with was a man whose praise mattered to me. What I got instead changed the way I viewed myself. This man, whose opinion I had regarded highly, told me that I did not run a mile that day. I told him again that I did, that I ran the mile and I finished it under time.

He repeated that I did not and further stated that he said he happened to be driving by the school earlier in the day and had seen me running. He saw me run a little and walk a little. He saw me run a little and saw me lean against the fence to catch my breath. He saw me walk some more and run some more and stop to huff and puff. He then told me not to go around telling people that I ran a mile when that wasn't the truth.

Looking back, I know that he was attempting to motivate me to do better and to push harder. In his way, he was encouraging me to not be satisfied with poor performance or to settle with just getting by. But all I heard in that moment was that no matter how hard I had tried, my best effort wasn't good enough. I had failed.

Sticks & Stones...

As my life progressed there were many times I would try hard at something and fail. We all do. It seemed like I would always go back to that moment in gym class where my best wasn't good enough and I began to identify myself as a failure.

Many times in life I had a full expectation of failing so I didn't bother trying. I made many poor choices based on the fact that "I'm a failure anyway, so what does it matter."

Every day, people are told things in life that are thoughtless, hurtful, and even dangerous. They're told things like "you'll never amount to anything", "you are worthless", "you are stupid", or asked "can't you do anything right?" They are told they are "too this" or "too that."

And too many people have made the mistake of believing those words and have allowed them to wound, hobble, and form in them until those words have become their reality.

...and Other Lies

For some people it's not words that have made them believe they are "less than". It is instead some other form of abuse, neglect, or even victimization they have experienced.

When those who are supposed to care for you abuse their power or fail to keep you safe, or when those who are physically stronger inflict their will on you, it tends to break something inside. The things that have been said and done to people because their worth was underestimated by others is powerful in shaping an unhealthy view of self.

If someone has caused physical, emotional, or spiritual harm to you because of their words and deeds, it says nothing about your worth other than they failed to take that worth into consideration. More than likely they didn't even recognize their own value. They couldn't give you what you needed because they lacked in that area themselves.

It's also likely that they didn't see that properly modeled for them. Hopefully this book will help some people change that cycle.

Perhaps it wasn't abuse or neglect at the hands (or mouths) of others, but your own mistakes. Even people who grew up surrounded by great and encouraging family, teachers, and friends can make poor life choices. Only one perfect, mistake free person ever lived and He didn't purchase this book.

People from all walks of life have momentary lapses of judgment which sometimes come with stiff penalties. Everyday people miscalculate and lose when it comes to risk/reward scenarios. Well intentioned but misguided people can follow their hearts toward disastrous relationships, bad business ventures, or failed experiments in life. That doesn't make those people failures.

Too many people have been scared by their mistakes into never trusting themselves or others again because the pain is too great. Too many believe the resulting consequences of bad choices is a lifetime of guilt and shame coupled with a belief that it is a forever price that we are required to pay. We believe we've made our bed and now we must lay in it and never look to make a change.

The thing is, our mistakes don't define who we are they define who we're not. The fact that we've recognized something as a mistake says that we don't identify with that mistake. If we don't identify with that mistake how can that same thing be a determining factor in our value? The simple answer is that it can't, unless we choose to allow it to do so.

Even natural life circumstances can cause us to think less of ourselves. Perhaps a job disappeared, or you've experienced an unexpected sickness, or the death of a primary loved one. These are traumatic moments in life that people experience every day, but sometimes the repercussions can be long lasting.

The financial impact, the emotional toll, the resulting loneliness, etc., over time can cause a downward spiral that makes us see less value in ourselves than what is truly there.

Whether it's the harsh words and actions of others, the choices we've made, or the situations beyond our control- anything that tells us we are of little or no value are lies. We often see our value in other people, things, or lifestyles and when we suffer a loss in one of those areas, we can believe the lie that our real value has been diminished.

As long as we believe those lies we will not reach the full potential hidden within us nor will we bring out the best in those around us. Relationally Driven people recognize their value is not determined by the words and actions of others, our mistakes, or life circumstances. Our value exists simply because we exist and if we exist, we have purpose.

A Tale of Extremes

Relationally Driven people are balanced on a humility/confidence spectrum. (See Fig 3 below) It takes resolve in who we are to ensure that we don't allow others to determine our value, even when we humble ourselves and put others first.

In my experience, I've seen that when people have allowed lies to influence their view of self they tend to go to one extreme or another. I call these extremes The Worm or The Bull. A person on the "worm" end of the spectrum may say or think things like "I don't matter", "I'm a failure", "I have nothing of value to contribute", "why try when nobody will appreciate it anyway" and so on.

They tend to feel as if they are less than other people, that they deserve the negative things that have happened to them, and that they will probably always be the lowest of the low.

The Worm mindset may come out in the form of not allowing one's self to dream or to pursue those dreams. It can hinder the presentation of helpful ideas and solutions. On the most extreme it can cause people to allow themselves to be victimized and even cause them to repeatedly return to their abusers.

People with The Worm mindset deny themselves and the rest of us the benefit of their potential contribution to this world. They don't allow their voice or their perspectives to be heard because they don't believe they have anything of worth to offer. If they don't believe they have them, they can't share them.

Because everybody has value, everybody has a purpose. The Worm mindset prevents that purpose from being explored and realized. The longer a person denies they have purpose, the longer those who would have benefited are denied. Relationally Driven people don't have a worm mindset. They have a healthy balance of humility and confidence.

On the other end of the spectrum is The Bull, who is very tough to be around. He says whatever is on his mind, he will have his way and not care who is hurt in the process.

The Bull says "I will make myself known", "I will be heard", "I will prove myself", and will run over whoever they feel they have to in order to protect themselves from ever being hurt.

People with The Bull mindset push others away. They are routinely abrasive, overall unpleasant to be around and difficult to get to know. In taking a bullish approach, they deny others the ability (or desire) to see their true value or the gifts and abilities hidden within.

As stated, we all have purpose. When enough people avoid us or don't enjoy being in our presence, our purpose goes unfulfilled. Relationally Driven people don't have the mindset of a bull. They have a healthy balance of confidence and humility.

Smack Dab in the Middle

Whether a person is on the worm end or the bull end of the spectrum, they have people at their home, on their job, and in their community that need them to change. We each have something inside of us that someone else needs. When we operate from one end or the other of these extremes, we deny others and ourselves of achieving maximum impact.

As I said in chapter one, whether it is creating profit on our jobs, healthy growth in our families, or seeing our dreams come to pass, we can't do these things on our own. We need each other to be the best people we can be and in order to do that we must evaluate where we are and make the necessary changes.

We must move beyond mediocrity and our status quo and push toward something better. If we are content being worms and bulls we will never get where we were designed to go or do what we were created to do. None of us want to get to the end of our lives and discover that we had an inherent value, but never used it to achieve anything great.

Relationally Driven people live in the middle of the spectrum with healthy balance of humility and confidence, between The Worm and The Bull. If they ever move left or right it is surely caused by a traumatic event not by the wavering of Relationally Driven principles.

Depending on which fear buttons are pushed or what memories are surfaced, all human beings have the potential to react wrongly. However, Relationally Driven people don't allow those traumatic moments to define them and they quickly return to the middle.

Relationally Driven people are not pushovers, nor are they overbearing. They are welcoming of others, even those who don't fit their own sense of "normal."

Relationally Driven people see the value in others and desire to add to that value. They recognize and celebrate the gifts and abilities of others without jealousy.

They are willing to provide constructive feedback when appropriate and to otherwise encourage and equip others to make the most of those gifts and abilities.

Even if Relationally Driven people don't know what their own gifts and abilities are, they recognize that they have them and work to discover, improve, and use them for the good of others. They readily evaluate feedback from others in order to improve but don't take that feedback personally or allow it to undermine their value.

Relationally Driven people are patient and kind to all people, not just those who are patient and kind to them. They don't put others down in order to make themselves feel or appear better.

Relationally Driven people are assertive, but they aren't rude or arrogant and they don't walk over people to get ahead. They think the best of others, even when those same people appear to be in the wrong. They seek forgiveness when wrong and make appropriate changes. They also forgive others who wrong them. They have healthy boundaries, but they don't hold grudges.

Relationally Driven people don't lie or gossip about others and they hope good things for them. They see the best in others, even when that best is hard to see, and they treat people according to that best.

Take a look at *figures 3.0- 3.3* (pages 49-52) and see where you find yourself. After you decide where you identify, ask two or three people their thoughts about where you fit.

They don't have to be those closest to you but should include some that are really close and some who are only casually close. Your response or feeling to their answers may even help you get more clarity regarding where you line up.

The Relationally Driven Humility/Confidence Spectrum

The Worm   Relationally Driven Person   The Bull

(Figure 3.1)

The Worm

- *Believes that other people have greater value, and articulates their own lack of worth. Seen as a pushover.*

- *Keeps ideas to self because they "aren't worth sharing."*

- *Dismisses own strengths and abilities and in turn fails to develop them which robs others of the benefits.*

- *Wears failures and hardships on their sleeves as proof of being unworthy of others' consideration.*

- *Lives in default mode and without purpose, accepts the "inevitability" of negative results, believes others are more deserving of and more likely to reach their goals and dreams.*

- *Lives at this end of the spectrum and only moves away from this end by crisis or encouragement.*

(Figure 3.2)

The Bull

- *Masks fears by expressing the greatness of own value while belittling the value of others. Often seen as cocky or arrogant.*

- *Endorses own opinions and ideas as the best or only option while others' points of view are not worthy of consideration. Volume is in direct relation to how "right" he believes his point of view to be and how well others submit or agree with that viewpoint.*

- *Exaggerates or hypes own abilities as an attempt to be seen.*

- *Wears past hardships on their sleeves as proof of how tough they are and how little they need others.*

- *Crushes tasks and goals in front of them, at the cost of discovering their own real purpose. Helps other people with their dreams & goals if it will benefit self.*

- *Lives at this end of the spectrum. Only moves toward the other end if moved by encouragement or crisis.*

(Figure 3.3)

The Relationally Driven Person

- *Equal parts confidence & humility; value is no less and no more than that of others, all people created equally.*

- *Readily offers thoughts and ideas, willing to be wrong, to compromise, and to learn from others.*

- *Develops and uses abilities to the benefit of others.*

- *Has a healthy transparency regarding own failures and hardships. Uses life experiences as learning tools.*

- *Finds joy while exploring and pursuing purpose, helps & encourages others in reaching for their goals and dreams.*

- *Lives in the middle of this spectrum. Can move slightly left or right depending on fears or crises, but recognizes the move and returns to the middle.*

Although some people live at the extreme edges of the spectrum, most are less defined. A person could be somewhere between the middle and the bullish side, depending on unresolved fears and frustrations. Someone may be mostly in the middle but have some "wormy tendencies" depending on past hurts and failures.

The point of this exercise is to see how far you are from where you want to be. It is that awareness and a desire to change that will help you get where you want to go. People who are Relationally Driven intentionally discover their weaknesses so they can make appropriate changes.

◆◆◆

Chapter Four - Authenticity Matters

Everywhere and Every Time

Have you ever accepted an invitation to a party, only to ditch that person for "a better offer?" That's kind of how I view our rejection of principles. A principle is a code that you live by even in situations in which you would rather not do so.

Living according to a principle is tough in the sense that when difficult situations arise we would sometimes rather behave in a manner more convenient than what our standard dictates. But principles do help us to make better choices in our lives even if they aren't the easiest choices.

The principle of authenticity says that we are the same person at home as we are on the job, as we are at school, as we are at church, as we are at the grocery store, as we are when we are stuck in traffic, and so on.

When we live by that principle the people around us get to know who we are and what we stand for. And really, we get to know ourselves better.

The Relationally Driven Approach dictates that no matter where we are and what role we are in at the moment, we treat the person in front of us as if they are worth our time and effort.

It doesn't matter if it's the employee talking to the owner, the customer talking to the customer service rep, or the parent talking to the child; every single contact we make with someone must take into account their value and our own.

Recall again the definition of Relationally Driven; living intentionally in such a way that people profit from being in your presence. The people who come near us should be better off for the experience. We can't control how they receive us but we can control what we give out in terms of adding to their value.

(Un)Masked

One recent summer I was walking through our local county fair and a young lady walked by me. She appeared to be in her late twenties, and she was wearing a black t-shirt with the words "That's Right, I'm a b____". I didn't spell out the word, but it rhymes with ditch. I'll let you figure it out.

The letters were big and bold and they were easy to see from a distance. She was walking with purpose and she was not smiling. She seemed to be making a statement; "stay out of my way!"

My first thought was "I bet she is a real peach to work with." But then I wondered if perhaps she was different person on her job. I pictured her as the front desk clerk at a hotel or a customer service rep in a call center. I thought that if she were to hold that job for any length of time, surely she would have to convey a completely different message about herself. Certainly she couldn't be employed long if she routinely told her employer, co-workers, and customers to "back off!"

A Relationally Driven person always sees the inherent value in others and in self and is lives in the middle of that humility/confidence spectrum, shared previously. But, too many times we put on masks and pretend to be something we are not in order to get by.

We believe we have to speak one way on the job and a different way around our friends, and a completely different way to the pastor or the elderly person next door. An authentic person "is who they is" regardless of what role they are in at the moment.

Does that mean, in the case of this particular young lady, that if she believes herself to be a "b____", that she should behave as such on her job, at home, and everywhere else she goes, in an attempt at being authentic?

No. It means that if she learned principles one and two, regarding her own value and the value of others, she would discover an entirely different way of presenting herself.

That's not to say that situational differences can't allow for different aspects of us to surface. For example, your job may require a certain amount of seriousness but a birthday party may allow your wild side to make an appearance.

Neither allows for the neglect or rude treatment of the people you cross paths with in either place.

The same goes for how you behave on social media, in traffic, standing in line at the grocery store. The principles contained in this book don't dictate the specific methods for treating others, but they do dictate that you see value in others wherever you are, and because you have confidence in yourself, you can treat others well without diminishing your own value.

If we are being inauthentic, that is, by demonstrating different levels of value, depending on who is around us, it's because we don't truly see the value in ourselves and others as equal. We either see ourselves or we see the other person with whom we are engaging as "less than."

We either believe that we have to hide who we really are because we are ashamed, or we don't respect the other person enough to share our genuine selves. Both of these instances require us to determine who we are looking down on, them or ourselves.

Through self-evaluation, input received from others, and by committing to make changes, it is very possible to make a significant improvement in your approach to others. Lifestyle changes are tough but the fact that you are here reading says that you are up for the challenge.

Another reason that people are inauthentic is because they are opportunists. They make believe they are something they aren't in order to gain. That's the total opposite of being Relationally Driven. Examples of this are evident when someone is kind to the boss but unkind to the subordinate or nice to a person's face but mocking when they are out of earshot.

Being Relationally Driven isn't about manipulating people so that you can get something out of them. That's what opportunists do. They see the strengths and weaknesses of others and play into them in order to achieve a goal. However, if your understanding about the value of people is something that you can turn on and off as it suits your needs, then you have no understanding at all.

The reason you are likely still reading this book is because on some level, you desire to make a positive impact in one or more areas of your life. Whether it be in your family, your job, your community, or your dreams, you came here because you want real change.

The only way that change will materialize is to do something different than what you're doing now. Recognizing the value in ourselves and in others is the catalyst for those great things to happen. At the end of this book, I'll let you know how to contact me if you would like some coaching in order make those changes.

Depth Determines Access Not Value

Being authentic doesn't mean treating every person exactly the same. There are different levels of relationship and those with whom we are closest should get the most access to our very best.

I can't treat my kids like they are strangers and I can't treat strangers' kids as if they are mine. That could cause real problems for someone. But just because someone is in the shallowest end of our relational pool or on the outermost fringes of our sphere of influence, doesn't mean they shouldn't at least get limited access to our best.

My wife expects kindness & patience but that doesn't mean I should avoid being kind and patient to others. I was told once that a person who is nice to his date but rude to the waiter is not a nice person. A Relationally Driven person is kind to both the date AND the waiter.

I recall several years ago, sharing with a small group of people about the importance of being on the lookout for opportunities to bless people who have needs. Immediately after our meeting, one of those families took my wife and me to lunch at one of their local restaurants.

As we were walking in the door I asked the raggedy dressed man holding the door how he was doing. He said that he was hungry and I said, "hmm" and continued walking inside. About three seconds later I was humbled as it dawned on me that I had just dismissed this hungry and more than likely, homeless man.

I was able to get a meal for him but the lesson stuck with me; I had seen him, but I hadn't SEEN him. I saw the shape standing there but because he was in the shallowest of all relationships- a complete stranger, I didn't immediately see the value in him. I very nearly missed the opportunity I had only moments before encouraged others to be on the lookout for.

Friendliness with the people you brush past in life doesn't cost anything but a moment of your time. Kindness to strangers, to co-workers, to the mail-carrier, it all matters and it's all part of being Relationally Driven.

Being Relationally Driven is about always giving your best to the people in front of you. Whether the best you have is a genuine smile and a kind word, the offer to help someone on your team carry their load, or holding the door for a stranger, seeing the value in others and recognizing that value in yourself opens the door for you to know what is best in those moments and helps you to walk through.

Chapter Five - Bringing It All Together

It's Not a Formula...

I'm hoping that you weren't looking for the 1-2-3 method for making people like you better. If there was a formula or a step-by-step method it wouldn't be truly relational, it would be manipulative.

Being Relationally Driven means that you approach people as the individuals they are not like dough where you can apply a cookie cutter process of engagement that gets the results you want.

Spend some quiet time thinking about the principles regarding the value of people, of self, and of being the same person everywhere you go. When you are cognizant of these principles it's much more likely that your approach to others will be in line with these principles.

If you don't take the time to think about them you will default to your normal pattern. It's about changing habits and we don't typically do that by accident. It requires intentionality.

When you think about the people with whom you cross paths, can you see their inherent value or are you fixated on what they can do for you and/or what they have done to you? If you can't address their value in the privacy of your own mind you can't really make the changes you need to make in order to get where you want to go.

Evaluate the encounters you had with people yesterday or last week and ask yourself knowing what you know now, what worked and what could have been done better. We can't get where we want to go if we don't know where we are or if we aren't being honest about our starting point. Remember this; your measurement of success isn't about getting specific results from someone it's about recognizing their value and adding to it to the best of your ability.

Intentionally (there's that word again) seeing the inherent value in people affects the tone of voice you use when you speak to them. It affects the words you use, the volume of those words, and the purpose behind them. When you see others as the awesomely created people they are and not according to that cost-benefit analysis you used to see them through, you set yourself up to give them your very best. But it won't happen if you don't make yourself evaluate your thoughts toward them.

When you think about yourself, do you recognize your own created value or do you still think of those things from your past as what defines you? Do you look at the circumstances you are in now and think about how much further ahead you would be if you had done things differently or had been treated better? Stop it! The past has nothing for you. "Woulda, coulda, shoulda, and if only" serve to keep us chained away from our future.

As you evaluate the way you think about yourself and your worth, if you find yourself focusing negatively on the decisions that you believe have caused you to be at this stage in your life, take time to forgive the person or people you believe responsible for those poor choices. Your choice is to forgive them (and yourself) and move forward, or to continue focusing on those things and staying where you are. As you read earlier, you may just determine to wear a mask to hide those thoughts, but eventually the masks have a way of coming off.

...*But*

Although there isn't a formula for the Relationally Driven Approach, there are some common things that you can keep in mind as you go through your day. This list is by no means all-inclusive. However, if you approach people with these actions in mind, it'll better position you to help others' to recognize that you value them.

> Use manners: "please" and "thank you" and the like go a long way. This tells the person on the receiving end that you appreciate their time and effort, whether they are simply doing their job or they have allowed you to do yours. Always express a genuine appreciation for the person in front of you. That word genuine is important. It helps you avoid sounding canned and rehearsed.

> Speaking of appreciating the time of others; be punctual. We seem to live in a culture that doesn't value being on time. You can say that you value people for who they are but making

them wait on you puts that into question. A singular instance of being late is understandable, a lifestyle of being late says "it's all about me."

Whether you are in a small group or a one-on-one setting, engage. When you intentionally remember the value of other people, you don't need to think of things like nodding your head, verbalizing agreement, or how long to look in their eyes. Just be mindful that allowing people to physically know that you see and hear them has the power to strengthen your connection. The more Relationally Driven you become, the more natural this becomes.

Learn to apologize, even when you believe you aren't wrong. You can be sorry if you (or your company) did something wrong, you can be sorry that something unfortunate happened to another, or sorry for their frustrations, inconvenience, a miscommunication, etc. There are lots of things we can be sorry for, and it's more effective when you see the value of others because they can then sense when your apology is sincere.

Acknowledge the feelings of others. Their feelings are their feelings even if you don't understand them. Blowing off the emotions of others can cause them to feel diminished while acknowledging them can add to their value. This isn't to say that you should allow yourself to be manipulated by the feelings of others, but be sure you don't swing so far to the other end that you become dismissive or patronizing.

Celebrate others. If they have a cause to celebrate, celebrate with them. I'm not saying to cheer on bad behavior or poor life choices, but I'm saying that if they win, celebrate. If they are excited because their favorite team won, celebrate. If their favorite team is an elementary school curling team, celebrate. Births, birthdays, milestones, victories, promotions, weight-loss, goals achieved, etc. When you see the value in others and are being intentional about adding to that value, your celebration with them draws you closer.

Mourn with them. When you become aware of a major loss in the life of someone in your inner-circle or the stranger in line with you at the grocery store; mourn their loss with them. A genuine "I'm sorry for your loss" to that stranger can go a long way for them, and sitting quietly with the people closest to you in their time of need says much about the value you see in them.

Smile. A genuine smile says you are happy to be in the presence of the other person. Even if you would rather be on a beach somewhere, you are currently with that person and their value means something to you, something enough to make you happy.

Look people in the eyes. It's often said that the eyes are the window to the soul. When you intentionally look into the face of another, you have a better chance of recognizing their value. It also opens the door for them to recognize that you've seen them.

The above are just general thoughts. Taking the time to really see the people in front of you can go a long way toward helping you know what to say and do (or not say and do). Your recognition of their value (every person, every time) will dictate your approach way more than any list could.

Standing Out

When you look back through the principles and examples in this book you would be right if you believed that living this way is certainly easier said than done. If it was easy, everyone would be doing it. Just imagine for a moment what your corner of this world could look like if people were living selflessly and sacrificially for others.

What could it look like if everybody was being encouraged by others to pursue their dreams or to have the daring to dream at all? What might it look like if there were an army of people actually giving their time, talent, and treasure for the furtherance of someone else's vision, while pursuing their own?

What if there was an explosion of people living a lifestyle of kindness, not because they could get something out of it but because kindness is contagious? I'll tell you what; this world would be in much better shape than it is now.

The fact that everyone isn't living this way is exactly why you are going to stand out in your sphere influence. Relationally Driven people are different than others. They look and act differently than everyone else. They see others differently than they are used to being seen. They are light shining in the dark and light attracts people who are tired of being in darkness.

No matter their background, social status, financial state or any other possible identifier, there are people all over this world crying out for this Relationally Driven mindset to invade their homes, jobs, schools, and communities. When you are the one answering that cry, you set the stage for amazing encounter; for them and for you.

When you are a business owner or manager who treats your employees according to their inherent value, you develop a team of employees who want to do well for you, their co-workers, and your customers. You'll also be able to determine which employees aren't interested in this type of culture so you can either train them or build a better team without them.

When you and your employees greet the customers walking through your doors like they could be your friends instead of people with money whom you can sell, more customers will walk through your door. And when you are the employee who treats those customers' well, who is known for going out of your way to help them, your boss will take notice. If he doesn't, your next boss will.

When you treat your spouse and children according to their value, you begin to propel them into a better future. Don't forget, a better future for them is a better future for you.

Even when hard times come, and they do come, when you are Relationally Driven you will find that you have developed a unified strength to get your family through to the other side.

When you see the value of the disadvantaged in your community or in this world, and you see your value and the value of those around you, there is a beautiful opportunity to build teams of people to help meet the needs of those disadvantaged.

Being Relationally Driven is not something you turn on and off, it's a lifestyle that has the power to improve every place you make your presence known. That's an awesome power to have and makes life worth living.

Perfection Not Required

When it comes to the worth of people, we must recognize that we have no more and no less than anybody else. Being Relationally Driven takes that equality into account and commits to treating others a certain way, adding to their value regardless of the way you may feel about some of the outward differences.

You are also committed to treating yourself a certain way, not neglecting your own created value. As you are nearing the end of this book you may think that it is impossible to live this way but that's totally untrue. Some days are harder than others but it is not impossible. Mistakes happen and there is a learning curve. The encounter with that homeless man at the restaurant helped me grow. It wouldn't have, however, if I didn't already have a lifestyle of being intentional.

Many encounters on my journey, the good and not so good, have helped me develop this Relationally Driven mindset. Relationally Driven people aren't perfect, but they are willing to change. The fact that you are reading this book says that you are interested in changing, so I know you can do this.

♦♦♦

Epilogue

Thank you for taking the time to read this first book in the Relationally Driven series. As some of you followed along, it is likely that you recognized many of the themes contained herein. Most, if not all, are principles contained within The Bible and the majority can be summed up with the "second greatest commandment; love your neighbor as you love yourself." The idea of treating people well has rewards, whether you choose to believe in scripture or not.

If you have found this book to be encouraging or otherwise beneficial, please consider a positive review on Amazon and a recommendation to your friends and teammates. That would help me a great deal.

For updates regarding future book releases, blog posts, or to discuss how to implement these changes in your life, business, or organization, feel free to email me at *contact@relationallydriven.com*. I'm available for personal coaching, group training, and speaking engagements. Also, please check out my website *www.relationallydriven.com* and/or "like me" on Facebook.

Lastly and most important; love the person in front of you, do good, and be well. D.

www.ingramcontent.com/pod-product-compliance
Lightning Source LLC
Chambersburg PA
CBHW031544210526
45464CB00003B/1140